AROUND TIVERTON

TED GOSLING

First published in 2004 by
Sutton Publishing Limited

Reprinted in 2010 by
The History Press
The Mill, Brimscombe Port,
Stroud, Gloucestershire, GL5 2QG
www.thehistorypress.co.uk

Copyright © Ted Gosling, 2010

British Library Cataloguing in Publication Data
A catalogue record for this book is available from the
British Library.

ISBN 978 0-7509-2948-6

Typeset in 10.5/13.5 Photina.
Typesetting and origination by
Sutton Publishing Limited.
Printed and bound in Great Britain by
Marston Book Services Ltd, Didcot

Above: The blizzard of 27 December 1962 brought arctic conditions to the West Country that remained throughout January and February, making it the most severe winter since 1740. It was during this winter, when the snow remained for over sixty days, that this photograph was taken of one of Kingdom's Tivvy coaches struggling through banks of snow on a road near Tiverton. (*S. Kingdom*)

Title page: The mayor and Corporation enter St Peter's Church, Tiverton, on Remembrance Sunday, 1977. Among those present were the mayor of Tiverton, *Mary Turner*, Philip Camfield, Messrs Sidney Cox, William Dunsford, Eric Shapland, Brian Homer, Derek Coulthard, Ewart Champion and Mrs Rena Hobson. (*Mary Turner*)

CONTENTS

Tiverton Town Football Club, 2002–3. Back row, left to right: Ben Harris, Danny Haines, Richard Pear...
James Mudge, Steve Overy, Luke Vinnicombe, Shaun Guff. Middle row: Dai Morgan (physiotherapist), Ma...
Aubrey, Steve Peters, Nathen Ridge, Stuart Fraser, David Steels, Rob Cousins, Kevin Nancekivell, Mike Perr...
(physiotherapist). Front row: -?-, Steve Winter, Martyn Rogers (manager), Jason Rees (captain), Marti...
Grimshaw (assistant manager), Chris Hollaway, Paul Chenelworth. Sitting in the front: the Mascot is Sa...
Butler. (*Tiverton Gazette*)

INTRODUCTION

Tiverton was founded by the Anglo-Saxons in the seventh century on a site between the River Exe and the River Loman. In 1106 Henry I gave this valuable manor to Richard de Redvers, whose son, Baldwin, was created earl of Devon. Baldwin built Tiverton Castle, which became the Redvers' principal residence and later that of their successors, the Courtenays, until 1539.

It was the Redvers family who founded the ancient borough which until 1885 returned two members of parliament. In the late fifteenth century the town grew rapidly with the help of prosperous merchants like John Greenway, John Waldron and Peter Blundell. One of the great benefactions of Tiverton is Blundell's School, founded in 1604. Sadly, in 1731 Tiverton suffered a great fire which destroyed most of its houses. One of the survivors was Knightshayes Court, now a National Trust property, which stands in a fine park outside the town and was the seat of the Heathcoat-Amory family.

The castle and the fifteenth-century parish church of St Peter are built on a cliff overlooking the river. The elegant windows of the church, its parapets and pinnacles, are a splendid sight. John Greenway was responsible for much of its adornment, with numerous carvings externally and in his eponymous chapel. During the seventeenth and eighteenth centuries the town became a considerable industrial centre in Devon; one of the last woollen mills was taken over in 1816 by John Heathcoat, a lace manufacturer from Leicestershire, who was driven out of the Midlands by the Luddites. The factory is still functional, and continues to dominate the town.

Tiverton's attractions today include the Grand Western Canal, which terminates on the edge of the town and was constructed under an act of 1796: it is now a favourite place for locals and tourists alike. The East Devon College of Further Education is also sited in Tiverton and has become a recognised education centre for the eastern part of the county.

This latest book provides a unique collection of photographs and pictures for those interested in the more recent history of Tiverton. It includes photographs drawn from family albums, local collections and professional photographers. Many have never been published before and the reader will be taken on a fascinating pictorial journey through the years. Ted Gosling has brought this collection together to form a permanent record of the town and its past. This latest publication marks another achievement by the author and adds to his ever increasing series of books covering his native county of Devon.

Roy F. Chapple
Former Devon County Councillor and past governor of East Devon College

Aerial view from West Exe, south Tiverton, looking east, in 1975. A disused railway line can be see
crossing the River Exe, which is now Great Western Way. The gasometer and gas works seen towards th
top centre have now disappeared from Blundell's Road, and pictured on the bottom left the former Exet
Inn is now a residential building known as Jubilee Place, which was completed in February 2003. (*Expre
& Echo*)

1

Around the Town

West Exe Corner looking north towards Heathcoat's factory, 1970. About this time redevelopment was due to take place and much of the area was demolished. St Paul's Street on the left, plus the then Department of Employment offices, escaped this redevelopment and became listed as part of a conservation area. (*Express & Echo*)

Print of John Heathcoat's Lace Factory and School, Tiverton, *c.* 1830. (*E. Gosling collection*)

Here is the Old Market Cross which was erected near Coggan's Well in Fore Street in 1731 and wa dismantled in 1783. (*E. Gosling collection*)

ore Street, Tiverton, *c.* 1899. Here, over a century go, Fore Street was a place where the good people of iverton could stand about and talk – a far cry from day's street. (*M.K.I. Webber*)

ore Street, Tiverton, in about 1900. Compare this photograph with the same street today: modern motor affic has brought many problems to both town and country life but this typical road at that time reminds of one of the advantages. The age when the horse was supreme was also a time when the streets were vered with droppings and it was almost impossible to cross the road without getting one's feet muddy. *lary Symons*)

Left: Phoenix Lane, Fore Street, Tiverton, pictured here in 1964 before demolition to make way for the present-day Phoenix Lane. (*Express & Echo*)

Below: Bampton Street, Tiverton, looking north, 1961. This street has changed dramatically, although Lloyd-Maunders butchers are still on the same site. Towards the top left, Batten & Thornes Garage can be seen. In the centre of the picture on the left-hand pavement, John Stag can be seen walking up the street having come from his office of Dobbs, Stag, Knowlman & Co, auctioneers and estate agents – now known as Stags. (*Express & Echo*)

Right: Here is the new welfare department at Heathcoat's factory in Tiverton, which opened in February 1961. It was formerly Heathcoat County Primary School, started by John Heathcoat to provide education for the children of his lace factory workers. Today it houses the flourishing factory shop. (*Express & Echo*)

Below: Fore Street viewed from Tiverton Town Hall, 1958. It was clearly all two-way traffic in those days. (*Express & Echo*)

Demonstration for higher pay in Fore Street, 1972. The café on the right-hand corner has long gone, and Atkinson, the TV people, closed the shop some twenty-five years ago. (*Express & Echo*)

Massive flood prevention work in progress at Tiverton in 1968. This was to prevent the constant flooding from the River Exe which caused damage to people's homes in the west Exe area. Note the two giant chimneys on the Heathcoat factory in the background. (*Express & Echo*)

ampton Street, 1977. This was Queen Elizabeth II's Silver Jubilee year and the Market House buildings are ecorated with flags and bunting for this occasion. The old Market House was built in 1699. It was altered 1 1971 and you can see from this picture that it now has an attractive colonnade with three shops and a estaurant. On the roof is a central tower, whose clock, black with gilt Roman numerals and gilt filigree, is ated 1731. (*Express & Echo*)

re Street, Tiverton, 9 June 1977. Tiverton's main thoroughfare was, until it became a one-way street, the wn's through road from Exeter on towards Cullompton and Taunton. (*Express & Echo*)

West Exe Corner, in 1978. The Department of Employment building seen here was formerly the Labour Exchange and in later years became the Job Centre. (*Express & Echo*)

Old Blundell's School, founded by Peter Blundell in 1604, is seen here in about 1960. Over a hundred years ago the school moved to the present site and has since greatly expanded. The building seen here was taken over by the National Trust but is not open to the public. (*Express & Echo*)

ourist Information Centre, moving into the former Devon General Bus Offices, *c.* 1985. From left to right
re: Margaret I. Webber, Els Horsey, Wendy Searle and Merriel Spencer. (*M.K.I. Webber*)

he new premises for the Tourist Information Centre in Tiverton was opened in 1985 by the chairman
the Mid Devon Tourist Association. Pictured here, left to right: Els Horsey, Margaret I. Webber, the
airman of the Mid Devon Tourist Association, Merriel Spencer and Wendy Searle. (*M.K.I. Webber*)

Looking down Bampton Street in 1981. The one-way traffic seen here now flows in the opposite direction (*Express & Echo*)

Gold Street, Tiverton, looking west into Fore Street, 1983. The shop fronts are virtually the same twenty years on. (*Express & Echo*)

erial view of Tiverton looking south, showing John Heathcoat's factory, July 1985. St Peter's Church can be
en across the river from the factory on the left. Note Exeleigh House in the grounds of the factory beside the
iver Exe. This is where John Heathcoat lived before building Knightshayes Court. The bridge spanning the
xe at the top of the picture carried the Great Western Railway line from Tiverton to Exeter. Now a modern
ridge, called the Great Western Way, carries the heavy traffic. (*Express & Echo*)

The bottom of Bampton Street, in 1985. (*Express & Echo*)

Bird's-eye view of Exe Bridge in 1985. The tennis courts on the right are no longer used and have becom
overgrown, but the markings can still be seen. (*Express & Echo*)

...ore Street, Tiverton, 1991. The Tivoli Cinema seen here on the left still operates today, although Dewhurst ...he butcher's shop next door to the Tivoli closed down not long after this picture was taken and is now a ...ard shop. (*Express & Echo*)

...st orders when Geoff and Jenny Parr closed their shop in Phoenix Lane, Tiverton. (*Express & Echo*)

Here is an excellent photograph of the Ford clock tower with Mallards Restaurant in the background, 200
Mr Thomas Ford senior, the founder of Thomas Ford & Sons, brewers of Tiverton, gave the town the cloc
tower, and the opening ceremony took place at 5.00 p.m. on Saturday 16 May 1908. The time for th
opening ceremony was specially requested by Mr Ford so that the working classes could be present. I do hop
that he invited them all back to his brewery to sample the beer! (*Photograph E. Michael: print from Mallards*)

Westfield House, once the residence of holiday camp king Billy Butlin, is pictured here in 1956 with one of Kingdom's Tivvy coaches parked outside. The house was pulled down not long after this picture was taken and the site is now the garage of Kingdom's coaches. (*S. Kingdom*)

The days when the Devon General and the Western National had a network of bus routes throughout the county were recalled when these vintage buses turned up at Tiverton bus station to give tours in about 1990. (*R. Ridgeway*)

The old fire station in St Andrew's Street housed the town's fire engine. Before motor-driven vehicles the original engine was horse-drawn. This photograph dates from *c.* 1990. (*A. Hicks*)

Roadworks in St Andrew's Street for the southern relief road (Great Western Way), *c.* 1994. Tivertc Museum can be seen far right. St Andrew's Street was being cut in half at this time. There is now footbridge spanning the Great Western Way, which opened in May 1994. (*A. Hicks*)

2

The People

Tiverton's last Borough Council, 1973. Seated, left to right, are: Bill Authers, Brian Homer, Sidney Cos, Eric Shapland (mayor), P.C. Greensmith (town clerk), Harold Shapland, Bill Dunsford, Charles Skinner. Standing: Bill Jones, Mrs Margaret Allen, Derek Coulthard, John Lake, Victor Broomfield, Vivian Scott, Ken Greenslade, Charles Noon, Frank Suter, Trevor Borden, Mrs *Mary Turner*, Henry Ayre, Cecil Phippen, Mrs Winifred Rooks, -?-. The pictures on each side of the stained-glass window were taken for cleaning during refurbishment of the council chamber in Tiverton Town Hall. (*Mary Turner*)

Above: The sleepy heat of summer can be felt on that hot afternoon in Edwardian England when Effie Howe (Mrs Ellicott) poured tea in the garden of Old House, Blundell's School, Tiverton. Effie Howe was the cook at Old House before the First World War. Among west-country schools none has attained greater celebrity than Blundell's. Among the school's best-known pupils were Archbishop Temple, R.D. Blackmore and Bamfylde Carew, who ran away from school to join the gipsies and became gipsy king. (*L. Ellicott*)

Left: Tiverton resident Emma Rapson, who died in 1925, is pictured here in a photograph taken in 1923. We are left with the image of a flawless face with the enigmatic smile of the Mona Lisa, captured exquisitely by Knight, the Barnstaple photographer. (*L. Ellicott*)

bove: Taken in Tiverton during the early 1920s, his unknown family is setting off on a journey in a Model T Ford. Henry Ford's Model T must be given the credit for being the car that brought motoring to the masses; at one point in the 1920s half the world's automobiles were Model Ts. The engine of this maid-of-all-work was a 20 h.p., four cylinder, 2.9 litre unit, cast in a single block with a removable water-jacketed head. The gearbox, which needed some under-standing before it responded to reason, was a pedal-operated two-speed epicyclic model. (*Mary Turner*)

ight: Mrs Cissy Howe (*née* Aplin), of the Fountain Dairy in Angel Hill, was the wife of Len Howe, the owner of the dairy. This picture was taken in 1948. Before the First World War, Cissy used to drive the Royal mail coach and horses from Bridgwater to Minehead. (*L. Ellicott*)

Before the First World War many people thought women were physically frail and only capable of light work. The war changed that and women were soon to be found engaged in some of the hardest and toughest physical labour. In Tiverton these ladies worked at the brewery of Starkey, Knight & Ford and are busy rolling out the barrel. Although this photograph is charged with life and atmosphere, unfortunately the ladies cannot be identified. (*Mary Turner*)

Left: Mr and Mrs Leslie Clapp with granddaughter Alison at a family wedding in about 1960. Mr Clapp served for many years in the Tiverton police force. He also served as an area officer in the Tiverton Special Constabulary. After his time in the police he worked for Devon County Council as a food and drugs sampling officer, as well as being officer responsible for swimming pool water, which he regularly tested and monitored. (*M.K.I. Webber*)

Below: Milkman Len Howe is seen here outside Tiverton Castle in about 1941, driving the first electric milk float in Tiverton. (*L. Ellicott*)

Tiverton Rugby Football Club Team in the 1948/9 season. Back row, left to right: Tom Mortimore (chairman), Charles Morrell, Roy Amor, George de Wolf, Dai Davis, Derek Parman, -?-, ? Baker, Jack Gallard, Derek Nott, Mr Duddridge (sponge man). Front row: 'Squeak' Squires, Brian Homer, Eric Shapland, Harry Tidball, Ken Holland, Freddie Cook, Tom Jenkins. (*E. Shapland*)

Pictured here in 1948 are members of the Exeter Inn Darts Team. Back row, left to right: Ernie Sanders, Tommy Miles, Jack Cuttrell, Sam Morgan, Les Dennings, -?-, Stan Everleigh, Bill Cottrell. Middle row: Harry Pengelly (with hat), Tommy Howe, Walt Newberry. Front row: Les Pearce, Charley Williams (captain), Bill Shepherd. (*Elaine Chidgey*)

The lads from the Barley Mow in Barrington Street stand in front of their coach for this memento of the pub outing in 1971. (*Elaine Chidgey*)

Another group of lads from the Barley Mow are celebrating a win by the pool team in about 1991. (*Elaine Chidgey*)

The Beatles, The Rolling Stones, Mary Quant and Carnaby Street were some of the icons of the swinging sixties. In Tiverton during the same period, two sixteen-year-old locals decided to get married and here on their wedding day are Roy Jenks and bride Linda Holley. The best man was Raymond Webber. The photographer certainly succeeded that day in capturing a period sixties wedding picture. (*O. Jenks*)

Judging by the cups they are holding, the Ladies Darts Team from the Hare & Hounds in Chapple Street had enjoyed a successful season. Among the players are: Beryl Roberts, Rene Hill, Mabel Cole, Loveday Hill, Chris Woodward, Brenda Hill, Hazel Rowlett and Mary Williams. (*Elaine Chidgey*)

Left: A touch of cross-dressing here in the Black Horse in about 1970, when well-known Tiverton character Charlie Stevens posed for this photograph. The lady holding the bowl is Mrs Olive Cox. (*Elaine Chidgey*)

Below: For local customers the pub is a home-from-home, not just a place to drink but a place for a quiet chat or a game of darts. The pubs in Tiverton have always catered for all needs and they still play an important part in local life. Roy Butt, who died a few years ago, was a regular in the Barley Mow in Barrington Street and is seen here in his favourite spot in about 1990. Landlady Elaine Chidgey can be seen behind the bar. (*Elaine Chidgey*)

Tiverton tennis hard courts, *c.* 1960. Note the town hall in the centre of the picture. The mixed doubles players are Geoff Pack, Rod Gibbons, Peter Wood, Bettie Delling, ? Manley and Josie Williams. (*Elaine Chidgey*)

The Revd Coyle stands beneath the buffalo horns at a function of the Tiverton Royal Antideluvian Order of Buffaloes, *c.* 1955. Members present include Sport Dummett, Harold Lee and Bert Osmond. (*Elaine Chidgey*)

The ladies of the Withleigh WI paid a visit to the Mayor's Parlour in Tiverton Town Hall in about 1976 and appear to be enjoying a welcome cup of tea. From left to right: Mary Orchard, Ida Gooding, -?-, -?- mayor of Tiverton Mary Turner, Christine Luxton, Hilda Orchard and Mrs Stacey. (*Mary Turner*)

Not everyone is happy about the pedestrianisation of our busy streets. Here in September 1994 local people threw a human cordon across Tiverton's Fore Street in protest against pedestrianisation. (*Express & Echo*)

The Tiverton Reed brothers, seen here performing at a local venue in about 1985, were well known for their act in which they entertained with hits from the sixties to the eighties. (*Reed Brothers*)

Members of the fundraising committee at the refurbished village hall at Sampford Peverell. The ladies are Marjorie Lewis, Pam Brealy and Mary Isaac; the men are Ken Hornsey (treasurer), Gordon Conn, Peter Goffin (chairman), Arthur Sharland and Allan Weller. (*Express & Echo*)

Left: The mayor of Tiverton, Mrs *Mary Turner*, launched an appeal in 1977 to raise funds for every schoolchild to receive a Silver Jubilee commemorative mug. This was the start of the Silver Mile of Coins. (*Mary Turner*)

Below: 23 March 1977 was the 100th birthday of this resident of Belmont Hospital, Tiverton. Celebrations included a telegram from the queen, a fine birthday cake and a visit from the mayor, seen here presenting the centenarian with a bouquet. Unfortunately the name of the lady is unknown. (*Mary Turner*)

iverton Rugby Club members' dinner with guests including the mayor and mayoress, Councillors W.R. and rs Mary Turner, 1985. Ted Crowe is on the extreme right. (*Mary Turner*)

eady for Business'. In this enterprising line-up taken in February 1988 were advisers for the DTI Enterprise itiative with Regional Manager Mr Ian Huke (centre with beard and glasses) at Tiverton. (*Express & Echo*)

Celebrations at the Country House Pub, *c.* 1979. This pub, which stood at the bottom of St Andrew's Street was demolished a few years ago. The then landlord, David Spencer-Jones, stands in the middle holding hi Great Dane dog with wife, Pat, beside him. (*A. Hicks*)

Whitbread in the Community, October 1992. Tivvy Hands, left to right: Ray Cottrell, Chris Hutter, Cli Middleton, Daryl Manley, Committee Chairman John Burton, Terry Murphy, Glynn Charles, Nigel Manl and John Webber-Rookes. (*Express & Echo*)

Many changes had taken place since the founding of Gribble Booth & Taylor in 1923. From the original three partners in Yeovil in the 1950s, this firm of estate agents expanded, and at the time of this picture in March 1986 had seventeen offices. David Mettam in the centre started the Tiverton office in 1963 and retired as group chairman when the firm was sold to Royal Insurance in 1987. Frank Phillips is on the left and Nick Seddon on the right. Nick Seddon continued in his own name and is one of Tiverton's leading estate agents. (*David Mettam*)

Tiverton and District Round Table chairman's night at the Fisherman's Cut, Bickleigh, 1968. Left to right: Paul Perriam, David Mettam and BBC TV/radio presenter David Jacobs, who in those days regularly stayed at the hotel en route to Cornwall for broadcasting commitments. The man on the right cannot be identified. (*David Mettam*)

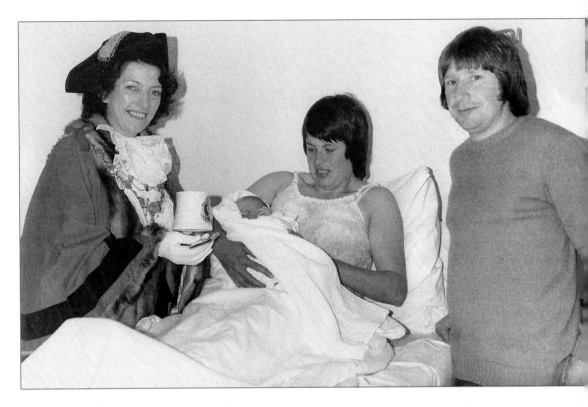

Above: Ann and Aubrey Harris were the proud parents of a baby girl, Kelly Louise, born on Queen Elizabeth II's Silver Jubilee Day, 1977. Mayor *Mary Turner* stands at the bedside to present a Silver Jubilee commemorative mug to Tiverton's newest citizen. The picture was taken fifty minutes after Kelly was born.
(*Mary Turner*)

'She must have been a beautiful baby'. To prove this Donna Kingdom poses with her mother Valerie, after coming second in a Tiverton baby contest in 1979. (*D. Kingdom*)

3

The Children

Above: Tiverton Girls Grammar School, Form VA, 1950. Back row, left to right: Margaret Clapp, Joan Colston, Phyllis Snow. Middle row: Mary Hunt, Valerie Doggett, Joyce Skinner, Sonia Potter, Maureen Cottrell. Seated: Mary Philp, M. Lanland, Marlene Hawkins, Peggy Drew, Gladys Pryer (form mistress), Hazel Webber, Margaret Heard, Mary Reed, Monica Hart. (*M.K.I. Webber*)

Overleaf: Days of innocence: the class of October 1938 at Tiverton Preparatory School. The pupils include John Lake, Dick Webber, Glynis Jenkins, June Burt, Joan Disney, Joan Wensley, Keith Brown, Dick Thorne, Dinah Edbrooke, Valerie Parminter, Bobby Lapworth, Molly Rumsby, David Gardner, Muriel Heard, John Hunt, Billy Gunn, Jennifer Webber, Mary Hunt, Tony Kitchen, Dawn Johnson with teacher, Miss James, and Headmistress Miss Tretheway. (*Mary Symons*)

Tiverton Girls Grammar School, 1948. Elizabeth Hager from the USA is taking a biology lesson. From left to right are: Joan Colston, Shirley McKee, Margaret Clapp, Mary Hunt. (*M.K.I. Webber*)

These boys from Tiverton Middle School are dressed in costume, probably for a school play, 1916. We only have the names of three in this group: Hugh Hunt, Chris Grater and Jack Vickery. (*Mary Symons*)

iverton Girls Grammar School hockey team, 1947. Players were, back row, left to right: Julie Stone, Shirley angdon, Sylvia Frost, Muriel Pengelly, Sheila Henstridge, Ann Darch. Front row: Pat Catell, Ruth Evans, Pat insey, Sports Mistress Christine Aze, Pat Fewings, Jean Heard. (*P.M. Shapland*)

ethodist Chapel social evening and supper. Among those present are: Mesdames Chambers, Beacham, app, Beale, Tancock, Brian King, Mary King, Marion Land, Alison Foster. (*M.K.I. Webber*)

1945 Middlemead Road (including Park Road and Park Close) party celebrations to commemorate VJ an VE Days. Present were: Messrs Morgan, Clapp, Brown, Marshall, Croker, Croxton, White, Potter, Bedforc Narracott; and children: Judith Brown, Judy Pither, Betty White, Keith Brown, Monica Bending, Mar Goodchild, Michael Parr, Dennis Croker, Margaret Clapp, Bobby Lapworth. (*M.K.I. Webber*)

The pupils of Heathcoat County Primary School, *c.* 1960. The Headmaster is W.S. Maddock. (*Elaine Chidge*)

Tiverton Show *c.* 1966. On that summer's day nearly forty years ago the generation that was to exhibit different attitudes in fashion, behaviour and thought were still children like these enjoying a day out. A way of life was coming to an end, and the photographer unwittingly captured a scene of innocence to disappear in the last quarter of the twentieth century. The children, members of the Veale family, were Jacqueline, Caroline, Rosalind and Anthony. (*C. Sapphire*)

The mayor of Tiverton, Cllr Mrs Mary Turner, judging a fancy dress competition to commemorate the 1977 Silver Jubilee celebration. (*Mary Turner*)

Silver Jubilee day, in 1977, brought a riot of colour, fun and excitement to the people of Tiverton. (*Mary Turner*)

Tiverton Silver Jubilee celebrations, in 1977. These children in the People's Park, Park Road, are waiting eager anticipation for the judging of their fancy dress competition. (*Mary Turner*)

he year 1977 marked twenty-five years since Queen Elizabeth II's accession to the throne. All over the Vest Country thousands of jubilee events took place, from sporting games, morris dancing and carnivals to treet parties, fireworks and fancy dress. Despite the rain clouds and cold winds, a massive show of loyalty o the Queen was shown by all. In Tiverton every street and road held a party, and here the people of Broad ane gathered to have this celebration photograph taken. (*Mary Turner*)

he mayor of Tiverton during jubilee year was Mary Turner, seen here standing on the left in her mayoral bes, judging a crown competition for children. (*Mary Turner*)

The proclamation of Tiverton fair, 1985. Mayor Ron Turner throws pennies to the schoolchildren. While the fair has long been discontinued this custom still takes place: the mayor throws hot pennies to the eager schoolchildren, who can keep as many as they can pick up. (*Mary Turner*)

The Tiverton sea cadets from training ship *Hermes* celebrate at their annual dinner, *c.* 1977. (*Mary Turner*)

Members of Newton St Cyres Young Farmers' Club with the cheque for £650 that they presented to Tidcombe Hall, Tiverton, on 6 January 1987. (*Express & Echo*)

Pupils from Castle Primary School, Tiverton, with a 'Food Through the Ages' exhibition at Tiverton Museum, *c.* 1990. Left to right are: Sophie Gibson (six), *c.* Dummet (seven), Samantha Hubbard (six), James Burden (five). (*Express & Echo*)

Above: The sad expression on the pupils' faces and the broken hutch followed the shocking discovery that someone had taken the Tidcombe Primary School guinea pigs, in June 1992. The children who looked after the guinea pigs, are, left to right: Emily Corbett, James Kearns, Sarah Mercy and Kim Creed. You can imagine they all have the same wish: 'we want our guinea pigs back'. (*Express & Echo*)

Left: A happy ending to the guinea pig saga is seen here when Sarah Flaws bids farewell to the two young guinea pigs she had donated to Tidcombe Primary School to replace the ones that were taken. The guinea pig minders were, from left to right: Hannah Marshall, Amy Gratten, Ben Corbett and Ben Murphy. (*Express & Echo*)

A Harvest Festival offering from pupils of Bolham School, Tiverton, in 1993. (*Express & Echo*)

Will you be Santa's little helpers? Tiverton youngsters meet Father Christmas beside the Devon General Santa Bus at Heathcoat School on 3 December 1993. (*Express & Echo*)

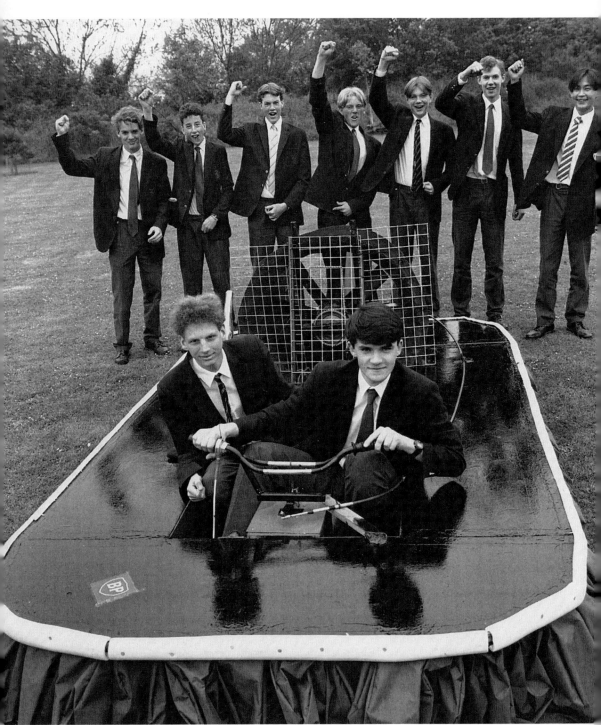

It was in 1958 that the British inventor Christopher Cockerell finally succeeded in getting official funding
develop his new hovercraft. The rest is history and its success proved that a heavy vehicle can be support
just above the ground or sea on a cushion of air. Here in July 1993 GCSE pupils from Blundell's can be se
enjoying the moment when they demonstrated the hovercraft that they had designed. (*Express & Echo*)

The famous Russell cross country runs are held at Blundell's School. In March 1995 the restored portraits of the Revd Jack Russell (founder of the races) and his wife were on display for the first time since they were donated. In the top picture the pictures are held by Paddy Armstrong, Director of Studies. Below, pupils from Blundell's School take part in the Russell. At one time this annual event was compulsory for all pupils, and when the River Lowman was in full flow many used to beg for sick notes from the school sanatorium to excuse them from entering the cold water. Swimbridge was Jack Russell's parish for many years and this famous hunting parson has long been a county legend. He died in 1883 after ministering in Swimbridge for half a century. (*Express & Echo*)

The Tiverton High School team who were in the 1998 Challenge South West and Wales Regional Final. From left to right: Michael Phillips (fifteen), Trevor Mills (sales manager from Richardsons of Tiverton), Matthew Bard (fifteen), David Lacey (service manager of Richardsons of Tiverton), Jack Vanstone (fifteen), Edward Smith (sixteen – holding the flag), Paul Crease (seated, head of Technology). (*Express & Echo*)

In June 1996 Two Moors Primary School, Tiverton, were joint holders of the Kingfisher Trophy with Ide First School for their wildlife project 'Birds on the Arm' in a competition organised by the Devon Farming and Wildlife Advisory Group. Seen here, left to right, back row: Clare Godfrey, Rebecca Palk and Laura Watts; front row: Sabrina Pengelly, Grace Cottrell and Wayne Broomfield. (*Express & Echo*)

ngela Browning, Conservative Member of Parliament for Tiverton, is seen here opening the new Tiverton Adventure Playground in Cowley Moor on 25 August 1992. (*Express & Echo*)

iverton carnival float, eptember 1991. Worzel ummidge and friends Tiverton Lions' Club ildren on this float – ere, left to right, Leanne arley (eight), Sarah Olsen ight), Christina Sanders ix) and Vicki Hadley as *orzel* Gummidge. (*Express Echo*)

Children of Sampford Peverell School who won a 'dog mess' poster competition organised by Mid Devon District Council in September 1996. Steven Harding, Melanie Tarr and Holly Sugg are seen receiving awards from Council Chairman Derrick Allen and Parish Council Chairman Richard Alford. (*Express & Echo*)

Pupils from Bolham Primary School get into a training walk ready for the Exmoor Challenge, March 1994. From left to right: Gavin Gale, Michael Phillips, Karen Rogers, Melissa Reed, Lizzie Parker and Charles Gold. (*Express & Echo*)

The mayor of Tiverton, Jane French, is pictured here throwing two-pence coins to schoolchildren during the proclamation at Tiverton town fair, Coggan's Well. This custom takes place on the first Thursday in June and October at midday. (*Express & Echo*)

Richard Holmes of Cullompton Antiques is seen here examining one of the valuables at an antiques road show with pupils of Heathcoat Primary School, January 1995. (*Express & Echo*)

Special Constables Tracey Standen and Tom Clow present cycling proficiency certificates to pupils of Coombe Mead Primary School. They are, left to right, Martin Slater, Andrew Empson, Esther Dyer, Karen Hagley and Kimberley Gibbons. (*Express & Echo*)

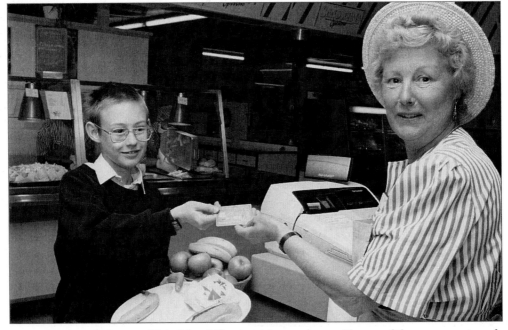

Kieran Bartlett of Tiverton High School (fourteen) is seen here with one of the new smart cards used to pay for school dinners with customer care assistant Jean Butland. (*Express & Echo*)

Headmaster Jon Statton with some of the pupils of Heathcoat's Primary School try to plot the route of the two whales the school has adopted, 27 January 1994. (*Express & Echo*)

Pupils at Bulham First School, near Tiverton, enjoying finding out what a real parachute looks and feels like, 3 July 1991. School Head, Mrs Margaret Herniman, said she became interested in obtaining a parachute after seeing one being used for a variety of purposes at a school in New England during a teacher exchange programme in the United States, which she attended about three years earlier. (*Express & Echo*)

Pupils at Tiverton High School with their certificates, and, centre, the branch manager of Tiverton'
National Westminster Bank, March 1993. (*Express & Echo*)

Pupils of Tiverton Heathcoat First School are seen here in about 1986. (*D. Kingdom*)

4

High Days & Events

VE Day street party at the back of St Paul's Church rooms on 8 May 1945. For the people here, as elsewhere, it was a time not just to celebrate but also to remember with pride all those who had rendered service in those dark days. (*Elaine Chidgey*)

Fore Street, Tiverton, 1908. All official parades in the town commence and end at the town hall, and election results are read on the building steps. Townsfolk have gathered in Fore Street in front of the town hall for many such occasions and this photograph shows such a crowd. Unfortunately the event is unknown. (*Mary Symons*)

Proclamation of the Fair, Fore Street, Tiverton, 1908. This traditional ceremony led by the mayor and Corporation takes place at Coggan's Well where the town leat, 11 miles long, disappears below ground before running into the River Lowman. Today the site is clearly marked near the top of Phoenix Lane. (*Express & Echo*)

tation Road looking from Lowman Green up to Canal Hill. Taken during the 1924 floods when the River
owman overflowed its banks, the GWR coal wagon is being used to convey railway passengers from the
tation to the drier parts of town. (*Mrs P. Gwilliam*)

bull-nose Morris car bravely tackles the floods at Lowman Green, 1929. (*Mrs P. Gwilliam*)

A water polo match between Tiverton Water Polo Team and the Devon Police Team in 1952 at Tiverton Swimming Baths. Among those present are: Patrick and Margaret Batting, Mrs Drew, Pat and Mrs Upham, Les and Edyth Clapp, Bet Winder, Mrs Hunt and Alan, Mary Stone, Mrs Millman, Chief Constable Ranulph Bacon and Superintendent E.J. Roper. (*M.K.I. Webber*)

Toc H Dinner, Tiverton, 14 January 1950. Among those present are Charles McDermott, Brian McDermott, Teddy McDermott, Rose and Joy Gray, Brian Hillman, Shirley Troake, M. Kerslake, Margaret Clapp, Ewart and Mrs Reed, Mr and Mrs Hillman, Ken, Brian and Mavis Greenslade, Mr Greenslade, Mrs Rowe and Mr Curtis. (*M.K.I. Webber*)

oung Conservative Party in the Small Hall, New Hall, Tiverton, 1950. Back row: John Lake, Geoffrey rown, Pat Nichols, Sonia Potter. Standing are: Jeannette Richardson, -?-, ? Mogford, Peter Higgins, Derek eal, Edward Stourton (wearing paper hat), Anne Fletcher, Mary Reed, Keith Brown, Margaret Clapp, alerie Doggett. Seated are: Peggy Wakefield, Janice Jarman, Nancy Horrocks. (*M.K.I. Webber*)

ecial Constabulary families sport evening held at Higher Moor Farm, Cowley Moor, in 1950. Running, ft to right, are: Mrs Davey, Clifford Williams, Mrs Williams, Christine Dadd, Margaret Clapp, Mrs Govier, -, Mrs Upham, -?-, Mrs Townsend, Mrs Goad. Behind: -?-, Dick Williams, Michael Williams, -?-, Terry wnsend and far right, David Down. (*M.K.I. Webber*)

The general election of 26 May 1955. The people of Tiverton are seen here waiting by Tiverton Constitutiona
Club, Bampton Street, to hear if their MP Derick Heathcoat-Amory, later Lord Amory, had been re-elected. Th
announcement that he had been re-elected was made from here, not from the town hall. (*M.K.I. Webber*)

The annual coach trip organised by the landlord was an event much looked forward to by local pu
customers. Jack Edbrooke, the landlord of the Barley Mow in Barrington Street, is seen in the centre of th
group wearing a dark jacket in this 1953 picture. (*Elaine Chidgey*)

A frustrating feature of the work of a museum curator responsible for collections of old photographs is the large number which bear neither date nor subject name. This picture is an example of this weakness. It shows the cast of a Tiverton pantomime, probably from the late 1960s. Any information would be welcome. (*Elaine Chidgey*)

Tiverton 'Specials' family party, *c.* 1955. Sitting, left to right: Les Clapp, Edyth Clapp, Police Superintendent Don Buckingham, Lionel Parminter, Clifford Williams, Mrs Upham. Others include: Elsie Wyatt, Doreen Ticker, David King, Alan Butler, David Down, Bill Upham, Mavis Thomas, Helen Goad, Mrs Goad, Mrs Kinch, Judith Kinch, Jill Cox. (*M.K.I. Webber*)

Crowds, including Councillors Frank Suter, Skinner, Cecil Phippen and Bill Dunsford, gather for the opening of the new bridge spanning the River Exe from Angel Hill to Bridge Street, 1968. (*Express & Echo*)

Mr Alex Cummings, exhibition secretary and youngest member of Tiverton Museum Society Committee (and director of Plymouth Museum), officially opened the Wagon Gallery which formed part of a £30,000 extension to Tiverton Museum, on 12 March 1976. The key is presented to him by Mrs Christine Field. Standing to the left is Mr W.P. Authers, curator of the Tiverton Museum. (Express & Echo)

Boys from Blundell's School help to prepare the Silverton village smithy, which had been donated to Tiverton Museum in its entirety. In the background are Alderman W.P. Authers (honorary curator) and Mr Alford (assistant honorary curator), 16 February 1978. (Express & Echo)

Tiverton Town Football Club supporters are seen here before setting off to Exeter in one of Kingdom's Tivvy coaches to cheer on the town's team in 1960. (*S. Kingdom*)

The ladies of Tiverton Soroptimists were present at this tree-planting ceremony. From left to right: Margaret Batting, Elizabeth Hill, *Mary Turner*, Mayor Harold Pennington (planting the tree), Dot Harris (president Tiverton Soroptimists) and Jennifer Pack, in about 1979. (*Mary Turner*)

Tiverton Buff Party, *c.* 1960. There are a number of sections or banners of the Royal Antediluvian Order of the Tiverton Buffaloes (RAOB), and while they differ in numerical strength and procedure all have the same purpose, 'the pursuit of brotherhood'. This is demonstrated in voluntary giving on such occasions as this. (Elaine Chidgey)

group of members of the RAOB gather for this presentation in 1955. The photograph is typical of its time and kind: essentially informative, it reveals the pride of achievement reflected in the faces of those present. (Elaine Chidgey)

Tiverton darts team at the Black Horse in about 1960. Among them are: Stuart Redwood, Arthur Redwood, Peter Davey, Tony Collard, Otto Buckingham and Terry Hicks. (*Elaine Chidgey*)

Reading of the Proclamation at Tiverton fair, 1976. This is a street scene of high quality with the Tiverton town mayor reading the proclamation of the fair as the focal point of interest. (*Mary Turner*)

An eagerly awaited annual event in Tiverton was the River Exe Struggle. This was a race on home-made rafts down the River Exe from Tiverton to Exeter's canal basin. The event was organised in aid of local charities. September 1969 saw the entry 'Up yer pipe I'm a plumber' and on board, left to right, are Mike Mingo, Mac Macdonald, Cliff Kingdom and Wally Richards. (*M.K.I. Webber*)

The Exe River Struggle, held in September, is organised by Tiverton Round Table. The rafts are made by groups of people and the race attracts entrants from a large number of local organisations. Visitors flock to vantage points along the route to witness the home-made rafts like the one seen here in 1972, paddled by, Mike Mingo (left), Anne Macdonald, and Mac Macdonald. (*M.K.I. Webber*)

HM The Queen Mother was always full of thought for others; she was deeply and genuinely interested in the welfare of the people she visited. This was reflected during the early 1960s when she paid a visit to Tidcombe Hall (a Marie Curie centre). (*Elaine Chidgey*)

Roy Waddington stands in the centre of what appears to be a retirement presentation at the Heathcoat factory, *c.* 1970. (*Elaine Chidgey*)

Fun in the snow was the theme for this tableau in the Tiverton carnival of 1949. On the flat are, left to right: Peggy Drew, Kenya Howe, Alan Howe, Margaret Passmore, Pauline Broomfield, Pat Pengelly and Maureen Howe. (*P. Ellicott*)

Directors of Medland, Sanders & Twose are seen here with Tiverton councillors in 1976. From left to right are: Philip Camfield (town clerk), Councillor Eric Shapland, Councillor Ewart Champion, Alderman William Dunsford, mayor of Tiverton Councillor Mary Turner, Laurence Tiltman (director), Sir Ian Amory (director), Councillor Derek Coulthard (half hidden), Bob Lockyer (director) and Councillor Ron Turner. (*Mary Turner*)

HM The Queen Mother has always been one of the best-loved members of the royal family, well known for her thoughtfulness and warm-hearted approach. The mayor and mayoress of Tiverton, Councillor Erick and Mrs Pat Shapland, were delighted to welcome her to the town on 1 July 1973 and she is seen with them here signing the visitors' book in the town hall. (*P. Shapland*)

The well-known band leader Joe Loss is seen here showing the mayor and mayoress of Tiverton his late record album when he played at the civic ball in October 1973. (*P. Shapland*)

The mayor of Tiverton lighting the beacon at Withleigh to commemorate HM Queen Elizabeth II's Silver Jubilee, 1977. Beacons were set alight to link up throughout the country to begin the celebrations. (Mary Turner)

Mayor Mary Turner is pictured here in 1977 accompanied by the borough beadle, Ron Butt, and the two mace bearers. The two maces of silver gilt are 3 feet 7 inches long and weigh, respectively, 102 and 114 troy ounces. In design and ornamentation they are identical, and were made in the City of London in 1727. The staff, carried in procession by the town beadle, is of considerable interest. Made about the same time as the maces, is a bamboo pole, 7 feet long, surmounted by a silver ball which bears the old borough seal. (Mary Turner)

Inauguration of Councillor Mrs Mary Turner as mayor of Tiverton in the town hall in 1976; her husban
Ron, became the first mayor's consort. (The first woman mayor had been Councillor Mrs Rooks, a widow.) Al
present are Joan Suter, retiring mayoress, Frank Suter, Bill Trickey, Vic Broomfield, Bill Jones and Ron Bu
(*Mary Turner*)

Vhere town meets gown, 1977. Mary Turner is seen here being welcomed by the Headmaster of Blundell's chool, Mr H. Gimson, on the occasion of Old Blundellians Day. (*Mary Turner*)

Alderman Brian Homer is pictured here holding his staff of office as bailiff of the hundreds at the perambulation of Tiverton leat, September 1989. With him are the 'withy boys' beating the leat. The perambulation of the leat is performed to preserve the town's right to the leat

given to Tiverton by Isabella, Countess of Devon, in 1250. At various points the bailiff of the hundred reads the proclamation. Withy boys (and now girls) ensure the water flows by stirring it up with their willow wands. (*Express & Echo*)

The opening ceremony of Ondaatje Hall, 15 September 1989. Christopher Ondaatje gave a generous donation of half a million pounds to Blundell's, his old school, after meeting representatives of Blundell's in Canada where he was living. This money was invested and when it reached a million pounds, this wonderful building was made possible. Seen here from left to right are: Lady Palmer, John Rees (Headmaster), Sir John Palmer (Chairman of Governors), Christopher and Mrs Ondaatje, Carol Rees. (*Express & Echo*)

In 1977, dressed in a nautical outfit, the mayor of Tiverton, with her consort husband and the deputy mayor and mayoress, Derek and Bunty Coulthard, paid a visit to HMS *Hermes* at Portsmouth. With a naval officer on either side, the mayor's party from Tiverton are, left to right: Bunty Coulthard, Derek Coulthard, Mr Turner and Mary Turner. *Mary Turner*)

iverton fire brigade rescue Father Christmas who
as stuck on the roof at Woolworths holding the key
e used to switch on the town's Christmas lights.
Express & Echo)

izabethan fayre in the Pannier Market in 1977. Enjoying an ice-cream, served by Dot Harris, the mayor is
companied by Chris Mumford on the right. (Mary Turner)

Perambulation of the leat, 1989. The 'beating of the bounds' with withies takes place every seven years along the 11 miles from Coggan's Well, Fore Street, to the source on Norwood Common. Representatives from local schools take part as well as local folk. Here we have Brian Homer (centre), bailiff of the hundred and his 'pioneers', leading the perambulation. (*Express & Echo*)

Old Blundellians gather for their annual Old Blundellians Day. Colin Beale, bursar of Blundell's and an Old Blundellian, leads the civic party towards the waiting group in about 1977. (*Mary Turner*)

Mayoralty room, town hall, Tiverton, 1972. Accompanied by her husband Ron, Councillor Mary Turner is presented to HM The Queen Mother, with the mayor, Councillor Eric Shapland, on the right. Behind Mrs Turner, Councillor Vivian Scott chats to Denys Rhodes of Uplowman House where the Queen Mother was staying. Denys Rhodes, now deceased, was married to the Hon Mrs Margaret Rhodes, niece of Her Majesty, and also a lady-in-waiting. Coincidentally, Mrs Turner and the Queen Mother were both wearing almost identical clothes – pale blue with cream accessories! (*Mary Turner*)

The mayor and mayoress of Tiverton with guests at the civil ball held in the Tiverton Hotel, 1986 (*Mary Turner*)

The mayor of Tiverton, Councillor Mary Turner, and Town Clerk Philip Camfield can be seen here at the Tiverton Hotel presenting a plaque of the Tiverton Crest to a visiting ladies football team from Swindon, about 1978. Replicas of the crest were given to all members of the team. (*Mary Turner*)

Christmas is a time for mysterious happenings and in every moment during the month of December something extraordinary occurs. Carol singers appear singing to the frosty night skies, a gay assortment of Christmas cards decorate the mantelpiece, shopkeepers keep us in a state of excitement as we prepare for the birthday of the Holy Child and in our towns the switching on of the Christmas lights becomes one of the most important dates in the calendar. The people of Tiverton all gathered here during early December 1988 to witness the switching on of their Christmas lights, and the joy they felt at that moment is reflected in their faces. (*Express & Echo*)

The League of Friends of Tiverton Hospital are seen here handing over a new hi-tech machine that will save doctors having to cut open patients in exploratory operations. The hospital consultant physician, Mr Harry Hall (centre right), is pictured taking over the machine from League of Friends Chairman, Mr Bill Trickey, with other medical staff and members of the League of Friends. (*Express & Echo*)

The chairman of Devon County Council, Mr Bill Evans, is pictured here planting a lime tree to celebrate the official opening of the Tiverton eastern distributor road during October 1986. With him are the chairman of Mid Devon District Council, Mr Derek Coulthard, seen to the left of the picture, and next to him stands the mayor of Tiverton, Mrs Eunice Hann. The chairman of the County Council Planning Committee, Mr Harold Luscombe, is standing on the right. (*Express & Echo*)

The Tiverton Round Table, Chairman's night, 1968. The outgoing chairman Paul Perrian is pictured presenting the chairman's medallion to David Mettem. Left to right: John Skinner (president of Tiverton Rotary), Jack Gould (chairman of Tiverton 41 Club), Paul Perrian, David Mettam, unknown. (© *David Mettam*)

Tiverton carnival tableau, 1991. The colourful spectacle of the carnival is as much a part of the Tiverton calendar as the seasons of sowing, harvest, Easter and Christmas. (*Express & Echo*)

The television presenter Martyn Lewis after unveiling a plaque at Tidcombe Hall on 23 January 1991, which commemorated a new era for Tidcombe following rebuilding work. (*Express & Echo*)

Lord Weatherill, fifth from left, at Blundell's School for a citizenship studies meeting, February 1994. Among those in the picture are Reg Waddington (managing director of John Heathcoat & Co.), Frank Rosamond (principal, East Devon College) and Robin Maxwell-Hyslop, MP for Tiverton. (*Express & Echo*)

Mary Turner, third left, with other members of the Tiverton Thursday Group, discusses their plans to launch a video to show just how vital the respite service is. (*Express & Echo*)

A scene from Tiverton Amateur Operatic Society's production of *Summer Song* which was staged at the town's new hall in 1994. (*Express & Echo*)

Pictured are Ray Hall (left), Hepco's managing director, and Paul Crease, curriculum team leader, design and technology, Tiverton High School. (*Express & Echo*)

The equivalent of the Football League's Cup Final is the Football Association vase which is strongly contested by amateur clubs throughout the country with the final at Wembley. The Football Association' vase was won by Tiverton Town during the 1990s and in the top picture we have the Tiverton player celebrating their win in the dressing room, and below some of the people who gathered in Tiverton to welcome the victorious players. (Top: *Tiverton Gazette*; bottom: *Miss Osbourne*)

5

They Also Serve . . .

A group picture of the Devon Yeomanry taken at a camp in Teignmouth, 1914. In the middle of the back row is Tiverton resident Walter Ellicott. During this camp, which lasted for a fortnight, soldiers would spend their days in drilling, route marching, manoeuvres and would finish with a demonstration of field operations. Little did they then realise that their playing at soldiering would soon be over and they would be off to fight the Kaiser's Army. Walter Ellicott, who was born in 1892 and died in 1977, joined the mounted section of the Manchester Police Force after the war and retired in 1942. (*L. Ellicott*)

Dr William Temple, Archbishop of Canterbury (1942–4), is pictured here addressing Tiverton factory workers at John Heathcoat's factory, 1944. During the Second World War parachute silk and camouflage fabric were manufactured at Heathcoat's. Religious talks like this with a patriotic flavour helped to lift the morale of workers during difficult times throughout the war. (*Express & Echo*)

Tiverton Troop of the Royal Devon Yeomanry, July 1914. The 1st Yeomanry Regiment was formed in Devon on 15 May 1794 and until this date had played a part in the defence of the realm. All this was to change in August 1914 when war fever swept through Europe like an epidemic and weekend manoeuvres became the real thing in the hell of such places as Mons, Gallipoli, Ypres and Passchendaele. Tiverton men served with distinction in the First World War and one of them, Corporal Thomas Henry Sage, was awarded the VC for his gallant action in the Battle of Broadseinde. (*L. Ellicott*)

Tiverton Borough Police Force, 1942. The force, which was the smallest in the country, was in being from 1849 to 1943 when it was amalgamated with Devon Constabulary. Back row: Constable Harding, Constable Howe, -?-, -?-, Constables Squire, Bennett and Clapp and Detective Constable Richards. In the centre is Superintendent Beynon, with his dog, and, left to right front: Constable Arthur Chidgey, -?-, Sergeant Galpin, Sergeant Williams, Sergeant Land, Constable Squires. (*M.K.I. Webber*)

ocal Special Constables had played an important role in the Second World War and here, at the
Var Memorial Hall in Tiverton on 3 November 1945, they join together for a celebration dinner. During
he evening a presentation was made to Superintendent B.M. Bequon. (*M.K.I. Webber*)

he Tiverton Special Constabulary dinner on 24 March 1949 was held at the Palmerston Hotel. The guest
honour that night was Colonel Ranulph Bacon, Chief Constable of Devon, who can be seen seated second
om the right. (*M.K.I. Webber*)

Tiverton Police and Special Constabulary dinner, 1955. Seen here are: L. Clapp, M. Roper, B. Stone, Bill Daniels, ? Perryman, Bill Dadd, Bill Grabham, D. Buckingham, E. Jarman, L. Kinch. (*M.K.I. Webber*)

Tiverton church parade, 1950. The three members of the Red Cross in the foreground lead members of the Tiverton Order of the Royal Antediluvian Order of the Buffaloes in this church parade. The Buffaloes resplendent in their aprons and insignia, are followed by the Sea Cadets. (*Elaine Chidgey*)

pecial Constabulary Dinner, 1950. Seated at the table are: Police Inspector Hocken, Alderman T.H. Ford,
'olice Superintendent Reg Annett, J. Morgan, E. Jarman, -?-, L.A. Clapp, -?-. (*M.K.I. Webber*)

iverton Special Constabulary, 1950. From left to right are: Assistant Area Officers Leslie Clapp and
 Morgan; Police Superintendent R. Annett; District Officer E. Jarman and Area Officer Lionel Parminter.
A.K.I. Webber)

The skill and dedication of the national fire servicemen during the Second World War must never be forgotten. They carried out many heroic exploits during the air raids and performed deeds of bravery comparable with their comrades in the armed forces. Fire fighters from Tiverton played an important part in the defence of Exeter against enemy bombing and have continued a dedicated service to the community since then in fighting fires and conducting rescues. In this 1950 picture you can see Tiverton firemen in action. (*D. Winstanley*)

A group of remarkable men were brought together for this photograph of the Tiverton Special Constable outside the newly occupied police station at Beechwood in the Avenue, *c.* 1950. The Specials receiv extensive training for their support of the police force and are often called upon to assist in work that ful deserves praise. (*M.K.I. Webber*)

Tiverton fire service dinner dance in the late 1950s. Standing, left to right, are: Mrs Slade, Jack Bucknell, Basil Pearce, -?-, Jean Pearce, Jim Broom, Myrtle Broom, -?-, -?-, Jack Angus, Mrs Gilbert, Cyril Gilbert, Ada Angus, Les Slade, Doreen Winstanley, -?-, Elsie Greenaway, ? Sowden, Ruth Williams, -?-, -?-, Mrs Hayman, ?-, Mick Winstanley, Bill Williams. Guests seated at the top table include Percy Sowden, the mayor and mayoress, Charlie and Mrs Skinner. (*D. Winstanley*)

Tiverton fire brigade, mid-1960s. Back row, left to right: Dave Roberts, Percy Bowden, John Bowden, Martin Harris, Stan Wood, Barry Sowden. Front row: Dennis Alderman, Gordon Tapp, Cyril Gilbert, Percy Sowden, Roy Willis, Jack Bucknell, Mick Winstanley. (*D. Winstanley*)

Above: Tiverton fire brigade in the early 1950s. Left to right: -?-, Fred Hookway, Cyril Gilbert, Bill Williams, Jack Angus, -?-, Roy Willis, Percy Hayman, Basil Pearce, Les Slade, Harry Pearce, Jim Broom, Fred Wood, Jack Bucknell, Percy Sowden. (*D. Winstanley*)

Left: Members of the Tiverton Territorial Army D Company. The 4th Devons played a part in the coronation of Queen Elizabeth II in 1953. Presenting arms in Hyde Park on Coronation Day are, left to right: Alan Disney, 'Bungy' Saunders and Laurie Ellicott. (*L. Ellicott*)

The Armistice signed on 11 November 1918 was a cause for great celebrations on the streets of Britain's towns and villages, although for many it was a time of sorrow; a time to remember loved ones who would never return. In 1919 Britain's most solemn memorial, the Cenotaph, was unveiled by King George V in Whitehall and memorials were erected in every town and village in Britain in memory of the men who fell in the Great War. Names of those who died in the Second World War would be added later. The Sunday nearest 11 November was set aside as a national day of remembrance and on that

day, in every part of the country, services are held to remember the fallen. In the top picture the mayor of Tiverton, Frank Suter, leads the Council on Remembrance Sunday in November 1975, and in the bottom picture the mace bearers lead Mayor Harold Shapland and Corporation to the Remembrance Service in November 1971. (*Mary Turner*)

They are all out of step except me – that seems to be the message from the little boy on the extreme left when men from HMS *Hermes*, exercising their freedom of Tiverton, were seen here marching through the streets in early April 1979. (*Express & Echo*)

A drink for the boys, November 1992. Cans of beer and lager were donated by Whitbreads, Tiverton depot, to refresh troops in parts of the world that other beers could not reach. A group of eighty men from 845 Naval Air Squadron Yeovilton left for war-torn Bosnia with the comforting thought of eighty trays of beer packed up in their old kitbags. (*Express & Echo*)

6

Around the Countryside

Above: Middle Hill Farm, Ashley *c.* 1935. From left to right are: Arthur Bray, Jack Loosemore, Reg Whitcombe. Relaxing with a jug of cider, these farm workers enjoyed a much slower style of country life than today. At the same time, the work was hard and the pay low, and it would be foolish to oppose any progress that helped to relieve what was sometimes a harsh existence. (*L. Ellicott*)

Overleaf: In many respects hunting has changed very little, and photographs of meets sixty years ago look similar to those taken in recent years: it is mainly the clothes of the spectators that help to date the picture. Here, in January 1937, the hounds meet at Blundell's School and Hugh Hunt, with four-year-old John Hunt and daughter Mary, two and a half years old, are pictured admiring the hounds. Boys from Blundell's School can be seen in the background. (*Mary Symons*)

Middle Hill Farm, Ashley, 1936. This is one of those nostalgic photographs that successfully captures a moment in a way of country life now passed. Grass for hay is ready for mowing in June or July and in those days used to be stacked into ricks. The traditional method of haymaking was very laborious. The hay had to be cut with a horse-drawn mower, then picked by hand with pitchforks and loaded onto wagons to be taken back to the farm and made into hay ricks. In this picture stands farm worker Mr Blackmore, pitchfork at the ready, standing in the centre. (*L. Ellicott*)

Middle Hill Farm, Ashley, *c.* 1934. Every farm in those days had its regular labourers who never thought of changing their places of employment. The farm worker was a sedate sort of person, patient and uncomplain-ing; working outdoors gave him contentment. Despite a hard life, labourers had a native sense of humour with an ability to see the funny side of life. These workers at Middle Hill Farm were certainly enjoying the job. From left to right, ? Gillard, Bill Ellicott, Jack Loosemore. (*L. Ellicott*)

Members of the Ellicott and Bray families enjoy a welcome break from haymaking during the summer of 1936. These people, like their fathers before them, lived in direct contact with the land and regarded it as the great benefactor. (*L. Ellicott*)

Effie Howe in Park Road, Tiverton, on Dolly, *c.* 1912. This was a common form of transport in those days, though getting the pony harnessed was much more time-consuming than getting the car out of the garage. (*L. Ellicott*)

The Fountain Dairy in Angel Hill was run by the Howes. Effie Howe can be seen sitting in the milk cart on the left and Annie Howe is standing in the doorway. Dolly, the horse, knew the round well and would move on, without further orders, to the next house on the run as soon as the milk girls got down to make the delivery. (*L. Ellicott*)

Above: Walter Ellicott holding young Robert Ellicott is sitting with Jack Loosemore holding little Effie Ellicott in 1925. The very ordinariness of photographs like this made many people throw them away, yet they are factually and visually important in allowing us today to share a moment in the life of country people long ago. (*L. Ellicott*)

Right: The Ellicott family, *c.* 1930. To be country born and bred counts for less and less today, yet the countryman's knowledge gained at first hand against the vagaries of nature is not a thing acquired by book learning. The Ellicott family pictured here farmed Middle Hill, Ashley, and like many small cultivators, they knew every inch of their farm. (*L. Ellicott*)

The farmers of Britain produce more than half of the nation's food and cattle are among the most valuable produce of farms in the British Isles. In the early 1950s when this picture was taken most farms in Devon were still small, 65 acres or less, but today farms are growing in size and declining in number and we are in danger of losing the countryside's most valuable asset – the small farmer, the man who moulded our Devon landscape. But here on a day fifty years ago it was not all doom and gloom, when the Withleigh Young Farmers Club were prize winners in the Devon class at Tiverton Market. From left to right are: A. Shapland, E. Shaplin and D. Ayre. (*Pat Shapland*)

Until the advent of the tractor, shirehorses worked the land, and although mechanisation reduced the number on British farms, some farmers still use them. Michael Mingo of Tiverton is pictured here at a horse show near Tiverton with two well-turned out shirehorses belonging to W. P. Mingo & Sons. (*M.K.I. Webber*)

OAPs Christmas party in Bampton, *c.* 1959. (*S. Kingdom*)

David Mettam (left) and Colin Howe (right) finishing their race in the mid-1960s in one of the Tiverton Round Table Donkey Derbys at the West Exe Recreation Ground. (*D. Mettam*)

Dunsabler Thorverton, *c.* 1910. Houses like this belong to the countryside; they are not obtrusive like so many modern dwellings, they do not dominate the landscape but are content to be a part of it. The chimneys seen here are typical of early Devonshire houses. They are great square things, quite plain except for a course of bricks around the top. (*E.S. Gosling collection*)

An Edwardian postcard view of the Washfield Weir. (*E.S. Gosling collection*)

Affectionately known as the Tivvy Bumper, 14XX Class 0–4–2T no. 1442 with the single coach auto train was caught by camera near Halberton Holt on the Tiverton to Tiverton Junction Branch on 1 June 1963. This engine was bought for the Tiverton people by Lord Amory in 1965 when the Beeching axe closed the line. It is now housed in Tiverton Museum. (*M.K.I. Webber: photo by W.L. Underham*)

Much has changed since this Edwardian postcard of Bickleigh Bridge appeared. The Trout Inn now occupies the thatched property on the left and the Bickleigh Guest Hotel operates from the house in the centre. (*E.S. Gosling collection*)

Above: Bird's-eye view of Sampford Peverell looking north towards the church and higher town, 197? Sampford Peverell was formerly regarded as a 'borough' on the strength of its two-day fair and weekl market. It is a charming village scattered over a hillside with a number of fine old buildings. In the midd of the picture you can see the Grand Western Canal running from Tiverton (left) towards Westleigh (right (*Express & Echo*)

Opposite, top: Hemyock station, 1906. The Culm Valley Light Railway from Tiverton Junction to Hemyoc closed on 31 October 1975, six months before its 100th birthday. (*Norman Lambert*)

Opposite, bottom: Hemyock market day, *c.* 1906. A quiet village at the foot of the Blackdown Hills wit the remains of a castle and a church founded by the Normans, Hemyock is pictured here on market da^ For centuries country people would come into Hemyock on this day to buy all they needed. This traditio began to change when roads improved and the railway and bus diverted trade to Taunton and Tiverto^ (*Norman Lambert*)

The Grand Western Canal was built in 1814 primarily for the use of the lime trade. It was in operation for over 130 years and its remaining 11 miles run through some of the prettiest country in Devon. In this picture, taken on 30 July 1994, Jim the shirehorse can be seen pulling the narrow boat to its summer stopping place at the Tiverton Canal Basin. On the boat are members of the Grand Western Canal Trust.
(*Express & Echo*)

In July 1974 the country was at its loveliest, and how better to spend time than on the horse-drawn barge on the Grand Western Canal. This canal is a haven for wildlife and the water supports an abundance of insects and other small animals. (*Express & Echo*)

During the summer months a horse-drawn barge can be seen plying up and down the Grand Western Canal, and here in 1978 we have Tony Stockwell with a gaily painted horse-drawn barge at Tiverton's canal basin. (*Express & Echo*)

Time for tea, 19 June 1992. A stroll in the sunshine past the thatched tea room at the Great Western Canal Country Park at Tiverton. (*Express & Echo*)

Holcombe Rogus church, All Saints, *c. 1935*. The village name of Holcombe Rogus dates back over 800 years, for it is named after the Norman nobleman Rogo. The church seen here has a panelled gable in the porch and the north aisle has a roof with carved bosses and figures of angels. (*M.K.I. Webber*)

Cadeleigh church in 1930. The church of St Bartholomew stands on a high ridge commanding fine views. It is a neat little fifteenth-century church, a rebuilding of a much older building, probably of the twelfth century. From west to east of the church runs a fine arcade of five bays. The Leach monument in the north aisle is magnificent. (*M.K.I. Webber*)

Knightshayes Court, 1960. Knightshayes Court was built between 1869 and 1874 by Sir John Heathcoat-Amory MP, the first baronet. William Burgess was the original architect although John Diblee Grace completed the work. It was given to the National Trust in 1973 by Sir John Amory, the third baronet. Knightshayes, now open to visitors, lies 3 miles from Tiverton near the village of Bolham. (*Express & Echo*)

Knightshayes Court, 1992. Gwen Britton, right of centre, a National Trust steward, is pictured here chatting to visitors in the morning room. (*Express & Echo*)

The opening meet of the Tiverton fox hounds at Calverleigh Court. The hunt master, Martin Scott, is in the centre of the photograph. (*M.K.I. Webber*)

Bickleigh Castle, 1989. Bickleigh Castle lies on the west bank of the River Exe and was a moated and fortified manor house. The Courtneys of Powderham once used it as an estate for their younger sons but it was acquired by the Carews in 1519. The property later degenerated into a farmhouse but was restored to its present condition after the sale of the Carew properties in 1922. (*R. Ridgeway*)

A tranquil scene in 1985 at Higher Bingwell Farm, Exeter Hill, with Tiverton in the background. The sheep taking shelter from the midday summer sun under the shade of the tree are still important to the success of the farmer, giving him an asset in meat and wool. (*M.K.I. Webber*)

ACKNOWLEDGEMENTS

I am grateful to the many people who have contributed material for this book. Particular thanks must go to the editor of the *Express & Echo* for allowing me to use photographs from the paper's archives. Thanks are also due to Chris Wright, without whose help this book would not have been possible.

I am indebted to Mary Turner for allowing me to use photographs from her collection and to Margaret K.I. Webber for the kindness shown to me when she produced much needed images to complete various chapters.

Special thanks must go to the following people without whose photographs and advice this book would not have been completed: Mary Symons, Elaine Chidgey, David Mettam, Eric and Pat Shapland, Peggy Ellicott, Steven Reed, Olive Jenks, Doreen Winstanley, Alan Hicks, Norman Lambert, Donna Kingdom and Caroline Sapphire.

Thanks must also go to Simon Fletcher of Sutton Publishing for his assistance, to Roy Chapple for his introduction and to Dr Frank Akerman for his advice. I am grateful to my wife, Carol, for her encouragement and assistance and to Heather Sanham who gave invaluable help in producing this book.

Many books, newspapers and organisations were consulted, too many to mention, but the following were a mine of information: *Tiverton Devon* by W.G. Hoskins, *Tiverton Past and Present* by W.P. Authers, *Tiverton's Industrial Archaeology* by Christine Edginton and *The Grand Western Canal* by Jean Hall and Joy Yeates.